BLACK WATER IN MILK GLASS

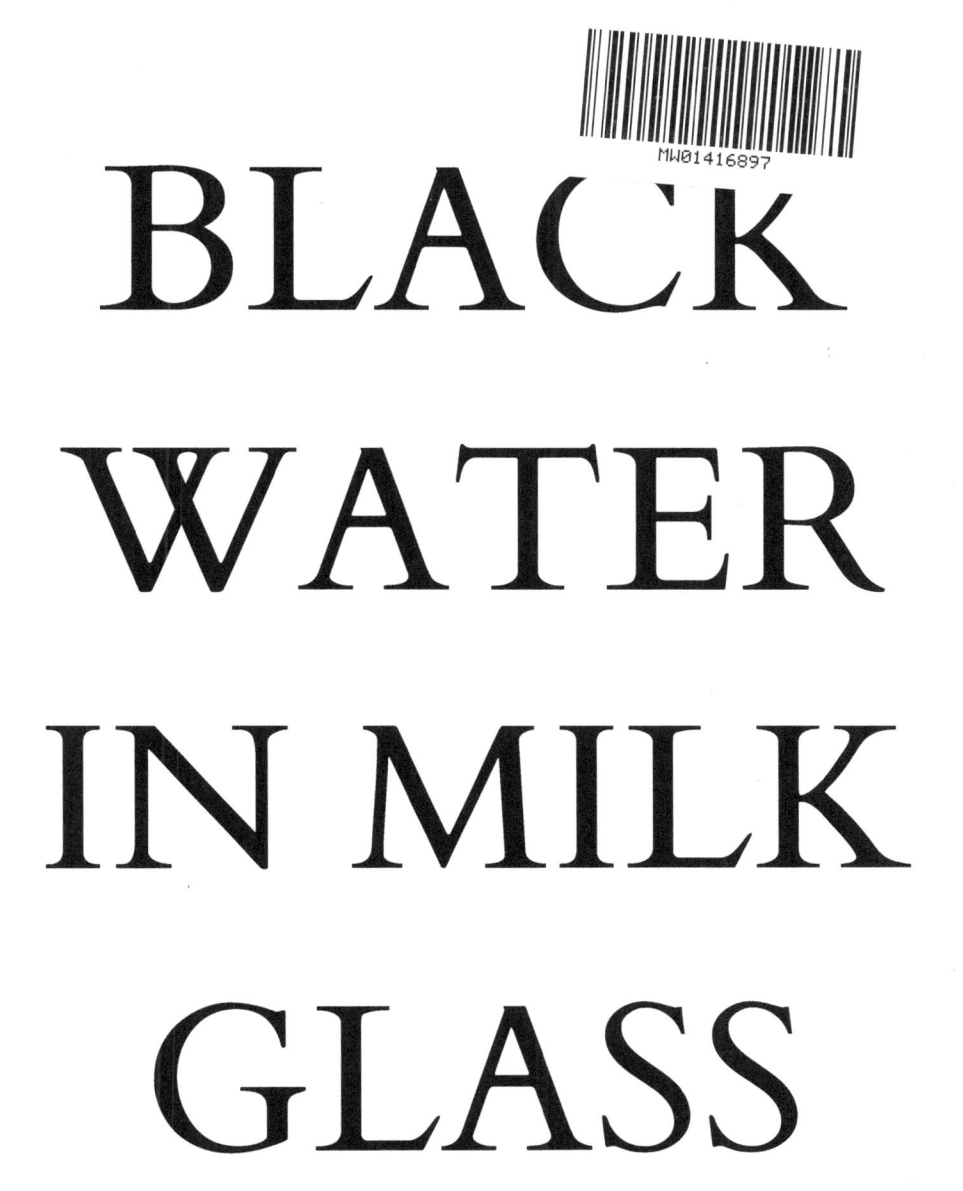

Poetry by Octavia Saturday

★ WEST VINE PRESS

THIS IS A WORK OF FICTION: Names, places and incidents are products of the author's imagination, and any resemblance to locales or persons living or dead, is entirely coincidental.

CONDITIONS OF SALE: This book is sold subject to the condition it shall not by way of trade or otherwise be lent resold hired out or circulated without the publisher's prior consent without a similar condition being imposed on the subsequent purchaser.

PRINTING HISTORY
First Printing, December 2017

BLACK WATER IN MILK GLASS is under copyright protection of West Vine Press and is intellectual property of Octavia Saturday & West Vine Press. Published by West Vine Press. Printed by LuLu Printing Company. The State of Michigan. The United States of America. 2017.

WESTVINEPRESS.COM

CONTENTS

- OVERWINTER EXILE (SELF-IMPOSED) 5
- LITTLE FALLEN ANIMALS ON THE FOREST FLOOR 6
- MATCHA, MELPOMENE, AND A LOVELY LO-FI BRAVURA 8
- THE LITTLE BLACK FLOWER HEART OF LISIEUX 10
- THE DAY THE CROWS DANCED WITH THE KRAKEN 12
- A TESTIMONIAL 14
- ALL WORK & NO PLAY, MAKES JENS A DULL BOY 15
- THE DEAD WILL LIE IN HONEY, BUT NOT TO ME 17
- NARCISSUS UNDEAD 18
- SALT & STYLE AND A FORCE RE-SUBMERSION 20
- BLACK WATER IN MILK GLASS 22
- QUEEN 0F CUPS WEARS BLACK OPALS IN HER HAIR 23
- REBIRTH, SYMBIOTIC TRANSITION 26
- CAUSE & EFFECT: AN EFFIGY 27
- UN DEUX TROIS; DEATH ON THE MOON OF PLUTO 28
- HELLMOUTH 29
- A TAOIST VERSION OF EVENTS 30
- TEXTING ABOUT ANAIS NIN, MERMAIDS & CIGARETTES 31
- A DELICATE HYSTERIA 33
- ADAGISSIMO 34
- THE IMPORTANCE OF BEING POLITE 36
- THERE ARE NO LOSERS AT THE EX-TABLE 38
- THE SKELETON IN E MINOR 39

INTEMPERANCE	41
TETE CAT IS MOVING HOME	43
KYOKO IN WONDERLAND	45
RYOKAN NOIR	47
INTERVIEW WITH POET	51
ABOUT AUTHOR	56
ABOUT WEST VINE PRESS	56
BOOKS IN PRINT (PUBLISHED BY WEST VINE PRESS)	56

OVERWINTER EXILE (SELF-IMPOSED)

The vampire twins retreat

To the warmth of east Indian welcome

Deep in the womb of the Egyptian teachings

Prayer and tea

We bring our understanding,

Conversation, philosophical meandering

We feed the feral cats outdoors

Let them in at night

Offerings to Bastet

We mind the time yet, always,

He watches the parameters.

Heavy bourbons made simple.

Make me a martyr?

No, never

I'm too small of bone, too fragile.

Fear, longing and fate.

Polite companions we are, always.

You have our sympathies

For the flawed perfection.

LITTLE FALLEN ANIMALS ON THE FOREST FLOOR

An infantile heart danced in the shade

Grandiloquent in its motions and games

Their moments carefully stolen

Confident in their deceptive sense of security

Movements unclean but steady

Glances guarded and guilded

Underneath a guilt of heavy tone

Blind lust propelled the cadence

Prior intention disguised as passing interest

A veiled scent of an escape route

That picked at the scab covering old wounds

Remnants of what little purity remained

Yet no one claimed love was fair

And traps were set on the sidelines

Sidestepped by the bystanders and out of sight

But the good ones gathered

Be they exchequer or executioners

Cheering on the downfall of our highborn shine…

Until our mutual tarnish was brought into the sun

And the prey animals caught their due notice…

Always is the way which came to pass

As nature is a hungry mother bitch

And a predator thrown as under

Is a dangerous heart to—break.

MATCHA, MELPOMENE, AND A LOVELY LO-FI BRAVURA

The boing water is tepid now

A lunar calm come over the looking glass

We wish

Together

Over pickled fish and plum wine

We've confessed our sins, our songs,

Our novella six dime store secrets

Penny dreadful villains

Whispering softly

Over green tea and overpriced sympathy.

Arranging the strands

For a better tomorrow amongst strangers.

A better shine for the shit shoes

These moments continue to unfold

We imagine our brunch

A wedded celebration

A shredded prism realized

Simplicity is the genius of the plan

From the last and until the end

This last call awakening is in motion.

THE LITTLE BLACK FLOWER HEART OF LISIEUX

Idolatry perhaps, but this is no schism

No error

Eros remains impure, imperfect,

Lovely and dreaming…

Brooding over the bloodletting and contagions

Of absence and pride

Oblivion and nuance.

A hibernation with the little queen,

A shovel for the girl in the box

To dig her own grave of renown

Or die in the trying

Birds aplenty to pick clean her bones

On a random winter morning.

There is no safety here

No illusion of muddied grace…

Only rusted signs on the sabbath

Flesh like candy clay

Porcelain once kept for prosperous evenings

Ripped open now and well spent

What propositions were made in the ether

What lies were solid

Insurance only as good as a wetted slip of paper.

Let us rest now.

The conclusion is incidental to the cause.

THE DAY THE CROWS DANCED WITH THE KRAKEN

Back on the esplanade,

Bookworms boiling

Like Taoist corpse oil

We cloister ourselves,

As spiders would.

Ancient eyes and cold of tongue,

Keepers of the stripped-down dream

Forage and stalk

Vultures circling the remnants

Of the rusted machine

Skills of fore thought and remembrance,

Litter the gilded poppy field,

And we burn

A relentless non-existence

In a nocturne voice

A solid structure of non-peril

Penitence for perfection

The owls call to the vultures and hounds,

Consume and vanish

A non-entity.

A TESTIMONIAL

A recollection,

8,000 out of ten

A memory of shattered symmetry

Silver sweet symbolic resurrection

This is merely a figment

Proof us a commodity in short supply and no demand

Truth abandoned

In the name of figurative peace

Auger your birds in the glass

Do they help, or personify hindrance?

Let them dance for you

Like a cheap Bangkok drug monkey,

Like broken nosed gutter clowns

Turn the corner, the tide,

Relax

Relax and go home, June

Our boy's been drunk again.

ALL WORK & NO PLAY, MAKES JENS A DULL BOY

The plea request fell on dark eyes and ears.

Recapitulate your own mistakes and dreams

No withdrawal shall be given at this date

Shear your own wool

Drain your own steel

This shark in the shallows knows no bounds.

Take all the suppositions and fuck with it

Like a knife

In your own beloveds back

This is no jest

Not a fucking video game. Not reality TV.

Phone your own journalists,

It's a competitive world

And everything counts in large amounts.

My judgement of flat back isn't quarrelsome

Shiny black just tastes better on the tongue.

This agreement of rabbis and sparrows,

Of the rabid, the adored, the numb

Counts for nothing

You'd have had to be there to seal the deal,

And geishas are never paid directly my love.

THE DEAD WILL LIE IN HONEY, BUT NOT TO ME

Black owls and brick dust

I'm the ace of spades

To the letter of the law

Instant replay of future's past

Bring it back round

Back to the charnel ground

Back to the scared source

Don't be cheap with the candy

And don't smell broke.

The significance here is not trivial

I joke with the charisma of Dracula shaman

Funeral rites in my head

Written on gray matter,

Branded on the blood.

Come see me sometime,

We welcome you in wonderland.

NARCISSUS UNDEAD

We gather in silence,

In dreams and games.

Splinter cells of wolves,

Calling out to a spider.

Connecting the dreamers and demons.

An objective to forage for,

Amongst the bones and stones,

Feathers and shells and shiny things.

So we'll say good night,

Good night and good luck

They told you to keep her

Keep he stars in your eyes and your gain…

Keep the pain and the spark.

Keep that which draws you

But your death hold weakens, by the second.

By the house, by the decade

A burning pool of what once was, soured now

A sanctuary turned toward suffocation,

Dim and unholy, both in word and deed.

So welcome to hell my love

A winter rive to cleanse the disease,

A frozen stream to carry you home.

SALT & STYLE AND A FORCE RE-SUBMERSION

A perfume so subtle

so as—to barely detect.

A horror so soft, so sweet,

So as—to barely dismay

The vultures are circling

A comeuppance for the queen of hearts,

And a backlash for the golden hen.

If I weren't a sociopath,

Id cry for us both

As it stands, no. never.

As it happens, feel free to dance.

No one is left alive to care,

No one left alive to die,

You're too late.

We learned all the lingo in our youth,

Us fox children,

Spirited away by the waves…

I recall myself as a kitten, lonely and obtuse,

Smelling the summons from beneath the waves.

Shall I recapitulate your lovely stitched whore?

Frankenstein organs and black button eyes,

I could smash her lovely empty skull.

I've done worse, as you know and adore.

Instead I abolish your sins,

Forget but never forgive,

And gave you your youth.

Still you smile to the sun

And pray bury me amongst the golden rod.

BLACK WATER IN MILK GLASS

We are the starved ones,

Dead and divine and dreaming of flowers.

I'll suffer the certain fate,

For prophets are shot in this time of lies.

Construct your honeycomb and lie in wait.

Wait like I wait.

Like an alligator in the shoal

Zen like timing

Mushin no shin

Perfection in the precision,

The self-assured vision

Instinct the only necessary tool.

Let the voices whisper,

Just return to yourself and rebuild.

Rebuild up remains

Your deconstructed towers.

Outlive your own autopsy.

And you see once again.

QUEEN 0F CUPS WEARS BLACK OPALS IN HER HAIR

There is a river rat

Come to pray at my veil

An attempted prophet

Loose in the sanctuary.

I won't be bothered to listen to the whispering,

But ill pour the pastis

For your lovely sunstone departure.

They come with absinthe,

With laudanum,

The willing and the brave

Come to drink from the spring,

The source

The secret.

Sip softly lovelies, and revel in the dusk.

Break an illusion of the lovelorn and lost.

For the broken winged will return.

Sit now and rest, you've done well…

I remain whole intact.
Halo shining and dark,
Unknowable as a nebula.
The dead we now know are pure and ready
both in sin and sincerity…

I've broke the bloodied, it's true.
Yet still the come to swim
amongst the in-between

Apothecaries full of reason and free advice
Like plastic cutouts of cheap Christmas witches.
But my strength never leaves,
dies or hides.
I remain.

Napping now and again

with a bull in the flowers

His familiar scent or comfort.

So, unlike the visitors.

The origin of where we differ.

REBIRTH, SYMBIOTIC TRANSITION

The stampede has run its course

The mermaid in fox fur rises

Like a black Madonna Venus in seashell

Botticelli dinners

Sushi on the corpses of dead girls

Rise

Shine and grind

Meditate

Don't lament what never was

Concentrate on what will become.

CAUSE & EFFECT: AN EFFIGY

Dissension

Pure

Dissect the inroads to a motivation

Rape art,

Die of the consequences

Fuck off

UN DEUX TROIS; DEATH ON THE MOON OF PLUTO

Bric a Brac…

Fallen…

From an empty winter shelf

They dust

They prey

They bleach.

Whitewash the bones.

A poor substitute but a solid investment

A settlement

A trade,

For the combustible crows, poor soul.

Penance for the true,

A black and blue tear

Your dime-store display of affection.

Give and take.

Win and…

Loose…

Stand in the corner until you can smile.

HELLMOUTH

Untouchable

Lascivious

In my absence, I abstain

From love, lust, from commerce, from life.

I'm auspicious,

A muse.

Broken doll caricature carcass

In women's attire

A cannibal

A demon dreaming of simplicity

In fair Verona

To sand to wind to ash.

There is no soil to escape to.

I'm a crook for life,

Murmuring the chant

Prescribed terms and lovely lies

Of death rattle night terrors.

Some love remains in my little teeth,

But I hold it alone.

A TAOIST VERSION OF EVENTS

Lemon and olive

Grange and Cardamom

Earthbound scents summon adhesion.

Until the projection takes shape

Takes meaning from illusion

And we take what we came for.

The tripartite equation

One

And the other

And the space in-between

Now lie in cruciform

Under the guidance of

Terpsichore.

Two agonic cygnets

Now bound

By illusionary sense of grandeur.

Bound by sinew

To the ten thousand things.

TEXTING ABOUT ANAIS NIN, MERMAIDS & CIGARETTES

Pour voir ce est le savoir, rapport a' l' auto

Semblable attire le sembiable

An emollient for the broken hearted…

"I've been underwater, and it's hard to breathe…"

Welcome to my world my one and only

The soundtrack isn't encrypted

But there's money to be made.

He came with a silver tongue inside,

Tragically insecure and vain.

A postmodern Byron in military boots.

Is hopelessness a metaphor?

Do owls swim, or skies fall?

Truth was a paradox in a paragraph

When a simple yes or no would have sufficed.

But we travel on, down the promenade

Snarling and sneaking but polished and awake.

Write the history on bone, pale and flat

Smelling of incense, oil and sweat.

Bowls of chocolate over conversation

Like child foxes in Grasse

After school and wearily eying one another

Flat black and shiny black, always together.

A DELICATE HYSTERIA

An unformed quarrel

Ripens from within

A byzantine opera

Of primordial proportion

The decision cast…

ADAGISSIMO

The molecules gather

Taken from

Bend and yawn

Perceive their existence…

Adagio Assai

The implications multiply

Interact and react

Perceive their strength…

Adagio

The schematics emerge

Stand and assert

Perceive their worth…

Adagietto

The decision casts

Peak and swell

Perceive its timing

Aria dentrata

The action unfolds

Refined and released

It has perceived its ability.

THE IMPORTANCE OF BEING POLITE

Hate has become a comfort

Hate across the board,

Equal opportunity

A cool hate, like marble.

Never gnawing, never boiling.

It remains mild mannered in my heart

Chopin Nocturne D flat Major op. 27 no. 2

Hate and death, mirror twins.

Hate and death, natural companions

Love, always the little sister

Lies asleep and dreaming

Hate and death Mirror twins

With grace and solitude,

I stand before you calm.

Blood Pressure non-detectable.

To stab someone in the throat

Or make a pot of tea is one and the same.

We are one, you and I, In our hatred.

We are one, and you know it.

So, let's smile then

For one another,

Eyes dead but sharp.

Let us smile and laugh softly

Over chaos's divine reign.

THERE ARE NO LOSERS AT THE EX-TABLE

Vague Colloquialism Past tense pyrexia, a filament.

Nothing more, nothing less.

Broken hearts are resourceful,

And we resolve to remain.

Unadulterated and unabashed.

Unavailing and unavoidable.

Rise up—

We are our own fetishes.

This fictitious dinner, merely a dream,

But no longer an issue.

To my betrothed in arms,

My beloved, No apology, no never.

I'm a fragile demon,

Evil from before you began.

So, I'll awaken the sleeping birds

As to know,

Where your truth begins.

THE SKELETON IN E MINOR

This passage down the snake track is unavoidable

so, let us follow

he moves ahead of me

to headed and glistening

sleep, writing down the oiled sand,

raw boned by the shore.

whilst the sun is platonic

I seek a darker understanding.

more akin to the lunar senses we share.

I've gambled

lied in wait in my time.

seen through it all like a gaze,

like fishnet, no matter.

for all is written, all has been said

nothing new is left alive.

nothing fresh to discover.

we merely rearrange information,

swap the strands.

reweave dead flesh to create the knowing

innocent blind grace

of the newborn demon

silently moving

without and within.

knowing that dead fathers deliver,

and this daughter of the crossroads

intends on being, paid.

INTEMPERANCE

We collide at times,

Drift and shift, intense, prodigal

We burn our intension,

Wide away like the shade of the sun.

Conflicts never born,

Of severity nor servility.

Not a figurative light or dance.

We greedily salt the wounds,

Piss on the open mouths of the grave.

A genuflection, perhaps,

Of our resilience.

"You have the stamina of a leopard seal"

He said…

"Even when you squander your seahorse heart"

Is this two-minded symmetry an insult?

Some days I've forgotten how to tell.

But we alone know the details by heart,

The final envelope of conditions,

Licked and sealed.

Is it a stamen or a truce?

Or a leftover helping of sleeping pills?

The truths and nuances and secrets,

We decide upon my love.

All I know for certain is we've won,

And the vultures always circle

To feast upon the remains.

TETE CAT IS MOVING HOME

Coquette has flown the coup

And the coronation in in full effect.

A quilt to construct, constricting

Piece by piece

Square by square

A five-point quarantine

For the serpentine kitten.

Submerged willingly

Spirit broken, for a time,

Yet clarity of vision intact.

I'm a thoroughbred.

A lightning storm cross the Mojave.

A libertine undead Lolita full grown,

Ever dangerous

Killing it hard and slow.

Out to move with the moon and tide,

To part the wine,

Out to blend blood.

Yes, my adored idol, my hated one,

What shall come shall be.

The lynxes paid.

The bourgeoise credit burned alive.

A billet-doux

A caveat

But I'm the honey in the sunshine.

Lush.

Pristine in my dented pale armor.

KYOKO IN WONDERLAND

There once was a little girl

Who had a little mark

Right in the middle of her forehead

Pale kisses made in parts

From with and to a broken skeleton.

Lovely and momentarily unspeakable,

A small story to write

In miniature from my toy sized tea house

A treehouse

From his queens own hardened blood.

So, we sit in the eye of the hurricane,

A picture near the window in the corner,

A print, a rabbit charm of truth

A record playing in the backdrop, repeating,

Napoleon less sphynx avee moi

By Henry Guillemin

The sounds sit in the air

Like a sheet of thin colored glass

Underwater I listen

Knotted tight and remembering

Let us speak now of secrets of the grave

Meet me on the corner of rue's

La Serene and La Lune

Your girl child is running wild now

Kitsune heart and cold heat scarred mind

Scarred…

But never

Scared.

RYOKAN NOIR

So, the quixotic arrives

Post the lords of the flies, past the sun.

Searching for complacency in the scarred skull

Licking my silver spine

Unnerved but shining

And I've always loved the shiny things

Our guided bones now in a lurid display

Flesh and calcium

Black tar ribcage.

I read these bones at long length.

Too hidden to see well, too strong to ignore

The crows gather and wonder

The slogans glimpse and vanish

Solve coagula

A cordon sanitaire

From the northern wind

A tiny dancing dream within a mantra

A mandala of living back sand

This confession has meant nothing.

THE MORBID LITTLE GIRL WHO BURNED DOWN THE TOWN

There is a Japanese assassin child

Who never grew up,

And her eyes echo across the ether

And at the center of the universe

Playwriters gather at the playground.

Mandibles in my hand.

This French made revolution.

Isn't up for discussion.

But shall this time be televised.

The favorable tides have gathered,

Time has snow drifted,

And cockblocked

Your hard copy candy shelf life

I'll apologize ahead my love,

But you've started to run your course.

This vision is close near murder.

Perfect, delicious, sweet in my mouth.

So yes, Delphi remains open,

And lovers always remember

The myriad of lost numbers left behind,

As dead and quiet as Pythagoras.

This impasse here, that obstacle there…

One may half close his eyes

To pretend he's dead

But we've too much style to notice

Or to return the gesture in kind.

So yes, Delphi remains open,

And I'm privy to the details.

Though, I've too much manners to be overly concerned.

INTERVIEW WITH POET

(WVP): Hello. Why is your name Octavia Saturday?

(OS): My name is Octavia Saturday because my birth number is eight in numerology. And the name Octavia both equals and means eight in certain hermetic esoteric circles and In Latin and English I believe as well. In short, eight is my favorite number. Samedi meaning, Saturday in French, is one of the Loa I work with. I'm a rootworker and a Vodouisant.

(WVP): What's so interesting about black cats?

(OS): Black cats are gods perfect little beautiful killing machines. I respect their hustle. I fuck with it.

(WVP): Coffee? Cream or Sugar. Or nothing?

(OS): Many creams and many sugars. I like it sweet and pale.

(WVP): What do you think about the future and technology and writing and life, the combination, when mixed?

(OS): I'm not answering this.

(WVP): Black water in milk glass. What does it mean?

(OS): Black water in milk glass comes from the most literal place possible. At the time I wrote this, I kept an altar with a milk glass dish of black water in it. I won't go into why, but I'll say that it was the best representation of my feelings at the time. Milk glass, by the way, is a Venetian blown glass that originated in the 16th century, I believe. If I remember correctly.

(WVP): Do vampires exist? Do ghosts spy on us?

(OS): Do vampires exist? Sure, in various forms. Literally even I suppose. Do ghosts spy on us? Wouldn't You?

(WVP): What is the most important, in your opinion, French philosophy?

(OS): Most important for France or to me? To France, I'd have to go with someone such as Jean Paul Marat, or even Robespierre. To me personally, I'd have to go with Sartre.

(WVP): Who are your influences?

(OS): It's a varried list. Burroughs, Anais Nin. Zazen. As far as Music goes everything from Joy Division and Sisters of Mercy to Throbbing Gristle, to Opera. The aghori. Siamese cats. Spiders. Basquiet. The French revolution. Chaos Magick. Aokigahara. Alligators.

(WVP): Favorite poets and writers, books, film, music?

(OS): I think I covered that under influences. But, I like to listen to Cold Cave a lot these days. I've been going through a moment with Cold Cave.

(WVP): Do you think robots will one day kill humanity?

(OS): Robots are the least of my concerns. I'm more concerned with the current farce of a presidential administration we have at the moment.

(WVP): Any plans for future books of poetry, are you writing now?

(OS): Yes, I am writing at the moment. A bit. We'll see what happens.

(WVP): Beer, wine, liquor?
(OS): I prefer opium.

(WVP): Hometown?
(OS): Kalamazoo Michigan.

(WVP): Night or day?
(OS): Night.

(WVP): Spring or fall?
(OS): Fall.

(WVP): Summer or winter?
(OS): Winter

(WVP): What's going on in the world, as far as society and in the world?

(OS): Well that's a broad question. There's a lot going on, per the usual. Most of which is of little use to me personally.

(WVP): Any thoughts on west vine press and the existence of the books and small indie book maker?

(OS): I'm a big fan of DIY and Independent, as far as Art, music, literature and culture in general is concerned. It's my preferred circle to be a part of, by far. It's far more visceral and just more interesting to put it simply.

(WVP): Anything else?

(OS): No.

(WVP): Give a favorite quote or line, just something you think could stick with the public.

(OS): "She keeps her Moet et Chandon in her pretty cabinet."

(WVP): Thank you.

ABOUT AUTHOR

Octavia Saturday grew up in SW Michigan. The great lakes. Water is a big part of her internal landscape. She writes about what is in her head that needs to bleed out. All the life experiences that have led her to where she's at and who she is. Octavia lived in quite a few places that have influenced her personally, and her writing, such as DC, Detroit, LA, New Orleans, Savannah, etc. These days she's happily back into her little wet corner of Michigan, where she's working on new poetry and prose that may turn out to be another book. Octavia can be found on social media at:
Instagram: @Laughing.Alligator.
www.facebook.com/octavia.gascogne.vonhauenschild

ABOUT WEST VINE PRESS

An Indie Publisher from Michigan that makes real books for real human beings.

BOOKS PUBLISHED BY WEST VINE PRESS

The Unbearable Heaviness Of Being Alive, by Patrick Trotti
Assorted Mental Ramblings Of A Sex Addict, by Jorge De Leon
Slow Living, by Kenyatta JP Garcia
They Say, by Kenyatta JP Garcia
Black Water In Milk Glass, by Octavia Saturday
Poetic Poverty, by Andrew K.
*Summer Of Chaos, by Andrew K.
*State & Stasis, by John Withee
*A Few Healthy Moments, by Rob Haskew
*The Napkin Book, by Jorge de Leon
*A Buddha Says Hello, by Sean M. E.
*It All Ends In Tears Anyway, by Patrick Trotti
A Flask of Gin, by Auden Wyatt
More Adventures Of A Dying Young Man, by Andrew H. Kuharevicz
Original Adventures Of A Dying Young Man, by Andrew H. Kuharevicz
The Fear & The Going, by Andrew H. Kuharevicz
*INDICATES BOOKS IN THE FUTURE DEAD WRITERS SERIES